Everything you always wanted...

Avraham Tzvi Schwartz

From the author of:
A Handful of Light ❀ The Need to be Great ❀ Hearts on Fire ❀ Keep Smiling ❀ Be Happy and Succeed ❀ Be a King ❀ Empowering Thoughts

Copyright © 2008, A. T. Schwartz

All rights reserved, including translation rights. This publication or any part thereof, may not be reproduced, or transmitted in any form or by any means, without prior permission, in writing, of the copyright owner. Small excerpts may be used for non-commercial purpose, on condition that the book's title and author are mentioned.

MELECH PUBLICATIONS
MESHECH CHOCHMA 27/3
MODIIN ELITE 71919 ISRAEL

Contents

Beaming 10
Now 11
Thank you.. 12
This is great 13
Everything I want 14
Love it 17
This is it! 18
Believe it 19
Focused 22
Self-wealth.. 25
More self-wealth 29
My reality 31
This is for me... 33
Oh yes! 40
This is for you.. 41
This is for us 43
Looking Upwards 49
Trust 55
I give you my heart.. 58
Despite it all 60
Forever 63
Endnotes 65

Using this book...

SELF-WEALTH

Everything you always wanted...

Alive

Waiting to Enter

Wondrous forces of healing, prosperity, harmony, friendship, insight and peace wish to enter this world. It's up to us to invite them in.

On the other hand, destructive forces, disease, poverty, corruption, violence, war and terror, likewise, wait to enter the world. Through neglect and cruelty, we allow them in.

Our destiny is in our hands.

Enjoy Life

For sure, life is about enjoying life. But we're never going to get there unless we learn how to enjoy more subtle pleasures.

So, for instance, we must learn how to enjoy:

- Our self-improved selves
- Helping others
- Doing what is right, honest, noble
- Meeting life's problems, challenges
- Details, quiet time, and more…

Fully Alive

If we live only to reach our goals, then we're only half-alive. We have to enjoy the trip as well – and to do this we need to focus on every step of the way.

Not Enough

It's not enough to strive for new heights; we have to enjoy the process as well. It's not enough to enjoy life; we have to reach for new heights as well.

Enjoy the Ride

We shouldn't forget – together with the 1001 things that are weighing us down, that we worry over and must deal with – that we also need to enjoy the ride.

How much passion

There are many elements of our life that we can do nothing to change, our age, our height, our childhood, etc. Other elements we can change somewhat, but not easily, our financial and social standing, personality, education, etc.

But, there is one element, the most important element of all, which we can and must control. This is how much heart we give to all we do, how much passion we invest in our lives. With this one element, we change everything.

A Second or Third Look

If an art expert urges you to look at a picture you don't like, you will agree to take a second look. If he tells you that it sold for $5 million dollars, you will take a third look as well.

The moments of our lives are also a creation, brilliant beyond any manmade work. Therefore, while some of them leave a bitter taste in our mouths, we should still take a second or third look at them. We may yet train ourselves to appreciate and enjoy them.

Aware

A thinking person is aware of the endless list of calamities that could have but haven't hit him at this time. As such, he lives this moment with heightened pleasure and joy.[1]

A Smile

One of the first things a baby understands is a smile. Doesn't that say something about the power of a smile?

The First

Be the first to say hello – to everyone to whom you can say hello.

Wearing a Face

Wearing a long, sad face grants victory over those who provoke us. Wearing a happy, smiling face grants us victory over those who antagonize us.

Now

A Determined Decision

Make a determined decision, right now, to be happy in this moment.

At the same time

At the same time, we can see the world in different ways. While we do not ignore the problems and challenges, the wars and worries that surround us – with those same eyes – we can also see the magnificence, the beauty, and the intoxicating happiness of it all.

Four or Five Words

Pick four or five words or phrases that sum up what you want from life. Now during your day repeat them. Repeat them that they burn in your heart. Repeat them that they reach the highest heights and rain down great happiness. Repeat them that they become your prayer.

Thank you

Exercise Gratitude

Say "Thank you, thank you, thank you," on and on, like a mantra, and as you do so let your mind scan all the things for which you need to be grateful.

Miracles

Our first step towards making miracles happen is to take pleasure from our lives, just the way they are.

Respect

The hammer cannot say, "I am better than the screwdriver". Even though that hammer costs three times the price, even though the carpenter uses it three times as much. Still, the screwdriver has unique features and abilities that that hammer will never reach.

This idea lies behind our ability to appreciate and respect every person in our lives.

When things are going well…

When things are going well, instead of expressing proper gratitude, we tend to tell ourselves, "I deserve that." And that's normally, when things stop going so well.

This is great

I love you

Empower yourself. Say-think to the Creator, "I love you." Say-think to everyone you see/remember, "I love you". This is a very powerful tool.[2]

To All

In your thoughts, say, "I love you" to the Creator of all. Say "I love you", to people you meet, people you see, people you know. Say, "I love you" to your world, to the elements of your world. Keep saying, "I love you", accustom yourself to saying, "I love you," and enrich your life.

Learn to Love

We have to learn how to love. We have to learn also, how to be loved.

Love Us

We all want others to love us. The rule to remember is that the more we love others, the more they love us.

To Feel Others

Aaah – to feel others, to hurt for their pain, to jump for their joy, to connect with them, care for them, worry for them as we do for ourselves, now that is greatness.

View Yourself

View yourself as a beautiful being, radiating love, understanding, happiness, etc. Keep this vision alive through your day, and live according to it.

Special

It's doing something extra – something no one else is doing – that makes us special.

Everything I want

Hunger and Pleasure

We only take pleasure from that which we hunger for – and the greater the hunger, the greater the pleasure.

Donkey-Rider

Our bodies are the donkey. Our minds are the rider. Now, let's get onto that donkey and ride it – wherever we want to go.[3]

Not Enough

It's not enough to wish for what we want. Rather we must reach for a goal, strive for a goal, holding it clearly in our mind such that we see it. Then, when we combine this vision with a trust that the heavens will help us reach our desires, the heavens do help us reach our every desire.[4]

Persistence

We need to pray and keep praying until we have all that we want. We need even to pray for the self-discipline to keep praying. For, what we persist in asking for, we eventually receive.[5]

Strongly Desire

It's not enough that we do what we need to do. We should strongly desire to do what we need to do. This energizes our personality, and adds beauty to our actions.

Desire

Desire is the root of all actions. [6] We need to know then, what our desires are, what our desires should be, and how do we harmonize the two.

Cleaner and Clearer

Desire is the root of all actions – and the cleaner and clearer our desires, the more powerful and effective are our actions.[7]

Not for the rewards

We shouldn't desire greatness for the rewards it brings us, but rather for the benefits, we can bring to our world and the people who people it.

Say Yes

Let's say yes to self-growth, to further study. Let's say yes to new challenges, new opportunities. Let's say yes to helping others, giving our resources, abilities and heart to benefit the members of our world.

Rise Above It

If they sling mud at you, rise above it. If they insult you, rise above it. If they block and interfere with your progress, rise above it. Be a great person.

Beyond

Rise beyond petty quarreling, complaining, resentment, etc., and move into a world of light, blessing and prosperity.

Love it

Busy

To survive, we must keep busy. To succeed, we must be busy. However, we should never forget in our busy-ness to take pleasure from the wondrous world we live in.

Higher Pleasures

Our lives include within them lower pleasures and higher pleasures. The lower pleasures are those of the body. The higher pleasures are those of the mind. We need to keep working on ourselves, strengthening ourselves, until our higher pleasures become the main pleasures of our lives.

If we were greater

We like doing the things we like doing. However, we should train ourselves to like doing the things we would like doing if we were greater than we are right now.

To be happy

We can be happy that we received an expensive gift or made a good deal. We can feel elated that we won a prize, loud applause and much praise. We can feel pleasure that we completed an important project and made a good job of it.

But the happiness we should strive for is the ability to take pleasure from doing our simple, everyday activities and duties. This ability is the highest achievement of all.

This is it!

Delicious Fruit

"A person is a tree of the field..."[8] and our children and students are our fruit. Moreover, all of our good deeds, kind words and beautiful thoughts are likewise our delicious fruits. The world is the richer for them – and we are the richer for enriching our world.

Good Music

A good musician produces music even from the poorest instrument. But someone who cannot play only makes a noise even from the best instrument.

So it is with life. If we learn and train ourselves to follow its rules, we produce music even in the poorest circumstances. But, if we ignore its rules, even under the richest circumstances, we produce no happiness or satisfaction at all.

Real Wealth

Real wealth is not simply having money and property, nor celebrating, spending and enjoying it. Rather real wealth is using it freely and generously to promote good in the world.

Believe it

Freedom

Freedom is the ability to live just as we want to live. The critical question is then, how do we want to live?

Limitations

Our limitations are not real. We can go beyond each one of them. And the place to start doing this is within our minds. This, after all, is our true reality.

Lofty Ambitions

Lofty ambitions protect us. They draw us away from ugly thoughts, speech and action.

Make way

Dismiss petty, irritating thoughts from your mind. Make way instead for elevating, empowering thoughts.

More, Less

The greater the person, the less he needs outside pleasure and stimulus to keep him happy.

More-Less

The more we bring the Creator into our lives, the more He is a part of our lives and the more He helps us. The less we bring the Creator into our lives, the less He is a part of our lives and the less He helps us.

The Right Buttons

By pressing the right buttons, we release heavenly blessings that allow our various projects to succeed. By ignoring these buttons, we stop these blessings from reaching us.

Among the buttons we need, are awareness, appreciation and gratitude.

True Success

There is commercialized definition of success. We dare not subscribe to it, for it leads only to frustration and despair. Instead, we have to understand and internalize for ourselves what true success is.

Choices

Which shirt would you like to wear, the parent asks the child, the green one or the blue one?

The Creator lays out all our options before us. He lets us choose. The issues however, are more serious than green shirts or blue shirts. For one choice leads us directly towards all we want, whereas the other leads us along a long, winding roadway with little satisfaction at its end.

With free choice

With his free choice a person can destroy, he can do evil. But, over time, months or even decades, this evil destroys that part of him that is evil and dies itself, leaving behind only what is good.

Attractive

With honest intelligence, we attract people to ourselves. With selfishness and greed, we repel them.[9]

Being Busy

Being busy gives us importance; being busy with something important, gives us more importance; and being busy with something important *to us*, gives us the greatest importance of all.

Give Importance

We need to give importance to what we count as important. We need to think through how we can best boost and make it happen.

Focused

A Good Intention

A good intention empowers us. The intention itself empowers us to carry it to its end.[10]

An Alien

To the live the ideal life, we need also to rise above our surroundings.

Imagine you are an alien, a visitor from outer space. On the one hand, you need to blend in with your surroundings; no one should notice you are different. On the other hand, you must focus and work towards your higher goal – to change this world for the good.

Minor Irritants

Minor irritants are good for us. They help us build resilience. To combat them, we block them from our thoughts – and in doing this, block out the world around us, and focus anew on reaching our goals.

Who are we feeding?

We need to ask ourselves through our day is who are we feeding? - Our lower-selves or our higher-selves?

Are we indulging our lower-selves – pandering to physical lusts and desires, bowing to lowly habits, allowing bad attributes, anger, jealousy, arrogance, silliness, depression, inactivity, etc. to take over our thoughts?

Or, are we feeding our higher-selves – learning new ideas, reviewing what we know, thinking, acting in noble ways, giving, forgiving, being grateful, loving, respectful, happy, etc.?

When we control who we feed, we control our lives.*

Only with Clarity

When we see the way ahead clearly, we should take it immediately. However, when we're not sure how to act, we need to pause. We need to check our facts, ask advice and think again before we take even one step in the wrong direction.

Our Own Behavior

Mostly we need to focus on our own behavior – our thoughts, dreams and plans – our words, actions, attitudes and attributes – our response to everyday challenges and

---

* Feeding our physical bodies can also be a form of feeding our higher-selves; this is when we eat with the intention that our food will give us strength to do all that we need to do.

difficulties. For, when we strive to be all that we can be, everything else works out around us.[11]

Questions

Here are questions to help us perform more effectively:

- How can I succeed better at doing what I need to be doing?
- How can I have more fun doing what I need to be doing?

Then, of course, we need to ask ourselves:

- What is it that I need to be doing?

Special Days

Special days make for special opportunities. We need however to make special efforts to gain their special prize.

Strong Determination

Keep your mistakes few and small. With strong determination and focus, you can reach all that you wish to reach!

What do I do best

Ask yourself, "What do I do best? What do I most enjoy doing?" Then, look to (1) steer your daily activities in this direction, and (2) do them with all your heart.

Your Best Option

We need to try always to do the right thing. It really is our best option.

A Clear Picture

Hold a clear picture in your mind of the person you would like to be. Then have this personality shine through you, through your actions and words.[12]

Self-wealth

Villain and Hero

The villain robs others of their wealth. The hero saves them from the villain. However, the true hero is the one who helps others to find the wealth within their selves.

Believe

To believe in something is to live it as though it was our reality. Then, in this way, it becomes our reality.[13]

Deep Thought

Sustained, deep, quality thought leads us to action – every time!

In Thought

Some people receive amazing salaries just to think. As for us, we likewise profit in amazing ways when we spend time in thought.

Mind-War

The hardest and most important war we fight is in our minds. Let's make sure to win it.

Pleasant Company

Pleasant company makes us feel good about ourselves; but we should learn to experience this same high from elevated thoughts.

Secrets

Life's simplest ideas – concepts and sayings we have heard many times – the attitudes and attributes we should be following through our days – are for us the universe's greatest secrets. For, while we give lip service to life's truths, we fail to internalize and include them in our thinking. Thus, their power remains hidden from us. They remain a secret.

Think Over

Pick a topic, a concept close to your heart. Find a quiet place, where no one will interrupt you, and think it over. Keep going as long as you can, five minutes, ten minutes, even more. If you're not tired, you will find that this exercise gives you the most energizing moments of your day.

Thinking Seriously

We can't do everything that we would like to do. Still, thinking seriously over what we would like to do, adds huge value to our lives. It is the first step we take towards being the person we would like to be.

Thoughts and Actions

Some of our thoughts and actions add to our lives, bringing us joy and riches. These are the thoughts and actions we need to promote. Other thoughts and actions sap us of life. These are the thoughts and actions we need to avoid.

Turn Your Thoughts

Turn your thoughts away from what is petty, small, beneath you, and focus instead on what is magnificent, awesome and reaches to the heavens. Think great thoughts.

More for our world

When we turn our thoughts to doing more for others, more for our world, when we cultivate a desire to contribute to our surroundings, we will find within ourselves new abilities and powers to do just this.

How He Works

We shouldn't be relying on our intelligence, nor our determination and strength, nor our wealth – but rather on our understanding of how the Creator works with us within the world. How do we access this information? – The first step is to ask, what is that we want from the Creator, and what is it that He wants of us.[14]

Don't be a fool

The first of the Torah's commands is don't be a fool.[15] Don't make foolish mistakes. We can control our stupidity by not acting impulsively, with bullhead confidence – pausing to think before we speak – and planning our lives in a deliberate way.

Nothing More

Do – all that you can do – and you have no more cause to worry.[16]

Faults and Weaknesses

We see our many faults and weaknesses as a reason to give up. But, our thinking should be exactly the opposite. This is something good! For, when we are conscious of our defects, we're already worrying and working on correcting them.

More self-wealth

A Garden

Our minds are a garden.

Certain thoughts, thoughts that shape our personality and character, dig up and soften our earth, readying it for growth.

Other thoughts, new ideas, or insights into old ones, are the seeds we plant in the earth.

Still other thoughts, encouraging, inspiring thoughts, water and fertilize our seeds, helping them to develop.

And the final product, the flowers and fruits, are the thoughts that lead us to action.[17]

Gift Thoughts

Large, beautiful thoughts attract large, beautiful gifts into our lives. Small, ugly thoughts attract small, ugly gifts into our lives.

Thoughts of love, respect and joy attract love, respect and joy into our lives. Thoughts of hate, jealousy and resentment, attract hate, jealousy and resentment into our lives. Why should we call that which is small and ugly a gift?

For, it too presents us with an opportunity to work on ourselves and grow.

Extra Cash

We need to feed our bodies. We also need to feed our minds. Which of these though do we feed with our spare time, our extra cash?

Goodness Entering

When we see it coming, it's coming. This is true of things we dread: "The thing the wicked person fears comes on him."[18]

Let's then dread nothing (besides doing wrong), and focus instead on goodness, blessing, prosperity and happiness entering our lives.

Hope

Sometimes we find it hard to believe that we will receive what we want. Still, we can, at least, hope and wait for it. We need to know that this hoping and waiting, this patience itself, releases great goodness and blessing into our lives.[19]

Not Enough

It's not enough to have a dream. Rather, we have to hang onto it with such determination until we become the type of people for whom such a dream is their reality.

Passion

If we can't be passionate about what we do, at least, let's feel passion about our dreams. This pushes our dreams into our reality.

My reality

A Watchful Eye

An athlete performs better under the watchful eye of his coach. Business people and actors also use coaches to help them reach their peaks. We too should make ourselves a coach. Let us have the heavens look down at all we do, guiding us with their approval or disapproval.

In the Mud

We cannot enter a banquet covered in mud. Similarly, we cannot enter higher worlds while lowly, ugly thoughts cling to us.

Magic in your life

Say, during your day, the words "Happiness and Joy … Happiness and Joy", a few times over, and bring magic into your life.

Say, during your day, the words "Love and Respect … Love and Respect", a few times over, and bring magic into your life.

Do the same for "Serenity and Peace", "Health and Power", "Affluence and Honor", "Wisdom and Self-discipline." Bring magic into your life.

No Mix

Nothing is so good that no bad is mixed into it. Nothing is so bad that no good is mixed into it. But, when we enter higher realms of meditation and thought, all is good and beautiful.

Pleasant Memory

Think back to a pleasant memory. Remember the place, the season and the weather. Remember the people who were there and maybe even the conversations that took place, the games you played and the food you ate.

Now think over the happiness of those moments, the excitement, friendship, harmony, serenity and peace you felt. These intangibles are the true greatness of that time. They are its spiritual components. They touch the heavens.

This is for me

Quantity and Quality

We can improve our lives materially. Likewise, we can improve our lives emotionally and spiritually.

We can improve our lives materially – working to enlarge our businesses, our assets and savings, the number of holidays we take, etc.

We can improve our lives emotionally and spiritually – working to improve our relationships with others, spending more time learning, thinking, appreciating the beauties of the world, etc.

The question is then where do we invest more of our energies?

A Ladder

Nothing is glamorous or exciting about a ladder. Still, with it we can climb to great heights. Similarly, little may be glamorous or exciting about the elements of our lives. Still, with them we can climb to great heights.

Small Errors

A fruit is its sweetest when it first begins to rot. We too can afford to make a few, small errors without this hurting us. Still, we must take care not to fall too far.

A Good Store

A store that sells the best products at the lowest prices doesn't need to advertise. People flock to it by themselves.

Similarly, when we possess excellent character and a willingness to encourage others, we have no need to promote ourselves. The people, who lead us to success, will find us themselves.

A Huge Difference

Look at a small child and see how his development, change and growth make such a huge difference in his life. Now, see this as possible for yourself as well.

A Step Forward

When we attribute our success to ourselves, we head towards disaster. But when we attribute our success to the Master of success, we take yet another step forward.

All Kings

We may not all be kings of our countries, our companies, or even our homes, but we can all be kings over ourselves. This is the secret of life, the secret of happiness.

An Opposing Force

We face an enemy. At every level, in every aspect of our lives, an opposing force blocks us from doing what we need to be doing. The only way to beat it is with awareness, thought and determination.

Bodies and Wealth

A car without a driver is useless. Similarly, our bodies without our souls, our life force, are useless. Still, it is our bodies that take us places; it is our bodies that help the soul accomplish great things. Similarly, the wisdom and material riches we accumulate help us reach new heights.

By working on…

By working on and improving ourselves, we rise above and escape many of the problems that plague our lives.

Cleanse Yourself

Cleanse yourself. Cleanse yourself of hatred, jealousy and anger. Cleanse yourself of complaint, resentment and looking down at others. Cleanse yourself of disappointment, aggravation and frustration, of feeling annoyed, ignored and insulted. Cleanse yourself and open yourself to miracles in your life.

Critical Moments

Five minutes in the presence of a king or a president can change a person's life forever. Likewise, moments of special energy, clarity, inspiration can charge a person's life. When such times come, we must be ready for them, take hold of them and springboard ourselves to new levels of achievement.

Flexible

Most of what we do is good. Some of what we do needs adjusting. Therefore, we need to be alert to what we are doing wrong, and be flexible enough to make the changes we need to make.

Generous Eyes

Elevated people look at others with generous eyes, seeing the good in them. Lowly people look at others with mean eyes, criticizing their every way. Let us pattern ourselves on elevated people, and learn to see the good in others.[20]

Hurdles

The higher we reach the more hurdles stand before and oppose us. Still, with determination and patience, we can fly over them all.

Instead of Waiting

Instead of waiting for wonderful things to happen to us, we need to focus on being wonderful people. Then, wonderful things will happen to us.

Likewise Man

The Creator can interfere and interrupt the natural running of the world. We call this divine intervention and miracle. Likewise, man can redirect the forces of nature to fulfill his personal dreams and ambitions. In this, he shares the qualities of the Creator; he creates miracles.

Help

The more help we receive in achieving all we want to achieve, the greater we are. Let's get that help.

Nobility

At times, unpleasant people, mean, petty cruel people, step into our lives. They upset, anger and depress us. Still, we should look at these moments as an opportunity to work on our nobility. We should see them as a chance to develop new inner strengths, the ability to remain cool and rise above small-minded people.

Others will notice

We cannot sweep our personal flaws under the carpet for too long. Eventually, others will notice them. The only solution, therefore, is to improve ourselves and clean them up.

On the Inside

We spend time grooming ourselves and dressing well that we should make a good impression on others. We should do the same for our internal appearance. We need to invest time and effort and be beautiful on the inside.

Our Mountain

To reach your goals is to climb a mountain. To climb a mountain you need to make a plan, to plot a route. Also, you need to ask others for their advice and help.

To Correct

A fault in ourselves we wish to correct is like any other challenge. We give thought to how we can best conquer it. We make a plan, sleep on it, pray for inspiration, and little by little, chip ourselves a tunnel through the mountain.

To Live with Ourselves

Our ultimate reward, as well as our ultimate misery, is having to live with ourselves – having to live with our attitudes and attributes – the person we choose to become.

Self-Advancement

We choose to focus either on advancing ourselves or that of a lofty cause. The truth is though we best advance ourselves when we reach for selfless goals.[21]

Maintenance, Growth

We busy ourselves with maintenance work and self-growth. We busy ourselves with maintenance work – eating, bathing, resting, earning a wage, paying bills, visiting doctors, taking breaks, etc. We busy ourselves with self-growth – study, contemplation, new projects, interesting challenges, planning, etc. The question is then, how much of our day are we spending on maintenance, and how much of it on growth?

Credit

While we all need some recognition, some approval, still by not taking credit for the good things we do, we open ourselves to great heavenly help.[22]

Half-dead

To be set in our ways, blocking all criticism and advice, and unwilling to change is to be half-dead. For our self-growth and greatness lies in us recognizing that we frequently make mistakes, and looking always to improve ourselves.[23]

Oh yes!

Live the truth

Live the truth, not because it saves you from problems, and not because it grants you rewards, but simply because it is the truth.[24]

Subject to Truth

We do not steal; we strive never to harm others. We honor our parents; we endeavor to honor others in our world. Because we know, there is a Truth higher than we are, and by subjecting ourselves to this truth, we connect and become a part of its eternity.

Pursue-Pursued

Pursue recognition and applause, and recognition and applause will avoid you. But look to recognize and applaud others, and recognition and applause will pursue you.

Pursue-Pursued II

Pursue comfort and prosperity, and comfort and prosperity will avoid you. But pursue the comfort and prosperity of others, and comfort and prosperity will fill your life.

This is for you

As many as we can
Ideally, we want to influence positively as many people as we can. With some people, we achieve this by drawing closer to them – with others, by drawing back.

Connect with Them
Ask others to tell you something about themselves, their day, and listen carefully. This will connect you with them in a powerful way.

Forgiveness
A great thing about asking forgiveness is how far it goes to empower others and boost their self-esteem.

Instead…
When someone counters our viewpoint with his own, instead of being aggravated, let's use it as an opportunity to praise him and boost his self-esteem.

Make way
Make way for others, step aside that their light may also shine. The gift you give them brings you a special reward.

New

A thought to run through our heads when we meet someone new is, "How can I help this person become better, happier, and more successful?"

Not Stupid

Be careful not to make others feels that you regard them as being stupid.

Small Gifts

There is joy in giving to others, even the smallest of gifts. Why don't we take more advantage of this simple device?

To Give

How do we give a gift to someone who doesn't know how to say thank you? We still give it, and some day he will learn how to receive, and give as well.

Up, not down

One of our great mistakes is that we look down on others – all others – instead of looking up at them.

Less Aggression, More Sweetness

We can deal with others with more aggression and less sweetness, or more sweetness and less aggression. We do better however, when we deal with them with more sweetness and less aggression.[25]

This is for us

I, You

I am you and you are I, and we are one – as long as we choose to see it this way. Let's be good to ourselves.*

An Example

Be an example of success, pleasant to all, happy and effective in whatever you do, and others will follow you.

A Great Exercise

Here's a great exercise. If you have someone who irritates you constantly, and you can't say anything about it without causing embarrassment, give a few minutes for a deep prayer that this might stop. Hopefully, you will experience something awesome. Either he will stop, or even better, his actions will stop annoying you, and you will have an extra proof of the power of your prayer.

---

* The Kotzker Rebbe would say, "If I am I and you are you, then I am I and you are you; but if I am you and you are I, then I am not I and you are not you." This however is no contradiction. A person should worry about his own self-growth. Still, such growth is only possible when we concern ourselves with the welfare of others.

A hint is enough

You don't need a sledgehammer to knock in a drawing pin. Similarly, when you deal with other people, a hint is often enough. We must avoid embarrassing others wherever possible.

Also You

The world around you is also you … as such, (1) enjoy the world around you; (2) beautify the world around you (at least in your thoughts), and (3) take responsibility for the world around you.

As One

Strive to be as one with your family and friends, as one with the world around you, and even, as one with the Creator of all.

As we look

As we look at others, let us see their depth, beauty, and even ourselves, reflected within them.

Condemning

When others hurt us, we need to be quick to forgive them – at least in our hearts. In addition, we need to ask their forgiveness, at least in our hearts. For, mostly, when we cry out against them, we condemn them beyond what is fair.

Fixing Others

We fix others by improving ourselves more and more.

For Others – and Yourself

Wish well on others – all others. Pray for their every success and happiness, good health, beautiful families, prosperity, etc. Do this especially for those who have most hurt you.

This is one of the best things you can do for yourself.

Give yourself a star

Count the times today others insult you without you insulting them in return, and for each time you win, give yourself a golden star.

Nice

If others are nice to us, this doesn't mean that they now owe us their friendship. Let's just be grateful for the time and care they did give us, and look for some way to please them in return.

Not Stupid

We may say and do stupid things at time, but this doesn't mean we are stupid. Let's do a better job now.

Others may say and do stupid things at time, but this doesn't mean they are stupid. Let's respect them better.

Our Challenge

We can't get away from self-concern, but we can make place in our thoughts for helping others and working towards a higher cause. This then is our challenge – how much thought to do we give to what lies beyond ourselves?

Outside Ourselves

We can't get away from worrying for ourselves. Still, our greatness lies in thinking of others and working towards higher causes. Interestingly, in focusing outside of ourselves, we really benefit much more than otherwise we would do.[26]

Responsible

We are, each, responsible for ourselves, for our growth, success and sense of satisfaction. We should be pushing to make it work for us.

As members of our communities, we are responsible for our communities, for their success and achievement. We should be thinking how we could bring joy to them.

As members of our people, we are responsible for our people, for their development and welfare. We should be praying for their success.

Special

We all need to be special. However, since we live in a sea of humanity, we do not achieve this so simply. Even when we amass tremendous wealth or fame, ultimately, these are nothing. Our solution therefore, is to be special in the quality of our lives – the quality of our thoughts, words and actions – the ways we spend the moments of our day.

Likewise, we are special when we help others feel special. This may just be the most special way of all.

We Assume

Naturally, we assume that those who hurt us do so intentionally; but most of the time, we are wrong.

Without hurting others

We can escape our worst heartaches without hurting those who brought us these heartaches. Let us pray that it should be so.

Likeable

We become more likeable when we like others. We should even try liking those people who don't like us.

Tolerance

The more we tolerate the shortcomings of others, the more the heavens tolerate our shortcomings and help us reach the success we want.[27]

What can I do

"What can I do to help others? What can I do to improve my world?" When we ask ourselves questions like these, we open our hearts and discover new talents and intelligence within ourselves.[28]

How popular

How popular would we be if we gave money to every person we meet. Well, we can do even better than that. We can help every person we meet feel important and good about himself.

Compassion

We all understand what compassion is. Now, we just have to practice it with others – even if we only do so in our thoughts – even if we only do a little bit more.

Gaining Friends

When we act selfishly, we lose friends. When we are giving, we gain them.[29] Our general intention should be then, that whatever we do should also benefit others.

Looking Upwards

The more...
The more we see the Creator in our world, the more we see the Creator in our world.[30]

All One
The most mind-blowing activity is for us to turn over in our mind the idea that the Creator is all One, and that every element of the universe is all a part of that One. This alone can keep us high for a lifetime.

Presence
A king's first, most important goal is to draw the Creator's presence into his self and his world.

A Measure of Success
Many people measure success by how much money they have or earn. Others measure their level of personal power and leadership skills, the influence they have over others, or how many friends they have. Alternatively, they measure their expertise and insight in their field of knowledge.

Still, the ultimate measure for all of us must remain, how closely do we connect to the Source of Life, in this world and beyond it?[31]

Plugged In

Even the best appliances need to be plugged in before they work. Likewise, we don't achieve anything without connecting first to the Source of all.

A Relationship

We need to keep building, adding to a dynamic, warm relationship with the Creator. As we pray, we should talk with Him – and as we think and learn, we should have Him to talk with us.

All

If the Creator is all, and the Creator is beautiful, then all is beautiful. If the Creator is all, and the Creator is good, then all is good. If the Creator is all, and the Creator is truth, then all is truth.

All from Him

Think about the Creator, for the goodness and greatness we possess, the power and the wealth that is ours, comes all from Him.

Endless

The Creator's power and wealth are endless. The only question is then, to what degree can we tap into it?

Every Moment

We need to be aware that every moment of life allows us to climb another step up the ladder of self-knowledge, mastering our world and a deeper relationship with the Creator of all.

Fingers

We can think of ourselves as fingers of the Creator, moving through this world, choosing to live, as He wants us to live.

Higher

The higher our thoughts, the higher we are. What are the highest thoughts we can think? – Those that concern the Creator of all.

Serve-Know-Enjoy

To *serve* the Creator, follow His commands, pray, do acts of kindness and learn his Torah, leads us to *know* Him. To know Him leads us to *enjoy* and take pleasure from Him. And to enjoy Him leads to every type of satisfaction and happiness.

Injecting the Humdrum

The greater the person, the more he injects the humdrum, the mundane, repetitive duties of the day with excitement and joy. And he does this by connecting with the Creator of all.

Into Yourself

Breathe in, deeply, and as you do so draw the Divine Presence into yourself. Breathe out, slowly, and as you do so grace the world around with the Divine Presence. Then, once you fill your reality with this beauty, return the Divine Presence to the heavens above.

Life's Purpose

What is the purpose of our lives?

For us: to learn to appreciate – each moment anew – the wondrous, brilliant works of the Creator, and thereby draw closer to Him.

For others: to teach them how they may appreciate the Creator's works, thereby drawing closer to Him – and thereby – drawing us closer to Him as well.

Look

To look at the world and see all that it lacks, makes us miserable.

To look at the world and see its beauty and wonder makes us happy.

Then, we may look at the Creator, and see the beautiful world and the many wonders He creates for us. This puts us at the highest level of all.

Maintaining our Relationship

We really have to work on maintaining and enhancing our ever-closer relationship with our Creator.

Present

The more we appreciate the Creator, the more He is present in our lives, and the more He helps us.

Present your plans

Present your plans, your projects, your work and your dreams before the Creator of all – that He may bless them with success.

Plans

The plans the Creator lays before us for our lives are superior to any plans we may hatch ourselves. Let's try then, as best we can, to follow His blueprint.

Success Depends

A person, who thinks that his success depends purely on his efforts and ingenuity, cuts the Creator out of his life.[32]

The Closer

The closer we get to living as the Creator wants us to live, the more beautiful we become.

The Window

The window is the connection, the bridge between Hashem and us. If you have a friend on the other side of a wall, it's hard to communicate with him – impossible to give him gifts or receive them – but if you can open a window between you – aah – now that's better.

Through your Windows

Become a vehicle for the Creator. Those who peer through your windows will see the endless power and beauty within you.

Ultimately

We can call it "world peace"; we can call it prosperity, happiness, love, a sense of content and wellbeing; but ultimately what we all want is that the Creator should dwell in our midst.

Celebrate

We celebrate the fall of evil in the face of goodness. We anticipate with joy that justice will ultimately come, rewarding those who were loyal to it.

Love

If the Creator is all – both inside and outside of me – and I love myself, then I love the Creator.

Trust

Currencies, Economies

Why must currencies fall, economies falter, assets depreciate and lose their value? It is that we may learn to look to a higher source of wealth.

The Source

The Creator is the source and owner of all wealth, power and genius. Thus, as we focus, connect and unite with Him, we gain further access to this wealth, power and genius.

All for our good

The Creator takes care of all of us, always. The good and the bad are all His work – and all for our good. Trust means you know and live this idea.

Our big question is though, how do we get the Creator to release the goodness and prosperity that we want from life?

We need to know that without our effort things don't happen. The world around us substantiates this; you work, you receive; you don't work, you don't receive. 33

The challenge is however, to see that while we must work, our work is not the determining factor. We work only to overcome our lack of trust. Everything we receive is only from the Creator. When we understand this, really understand this, we will find that even a minimum amount of work releases to us everything we have ever desired.

Engrained Belief

If we believe we need to work an eighteen-hour day to make it, then we need an eighteen-hour day to make it. If we believe we need an eight-hour day to make it, then we need eight-hour day to make it. If we believe we need a three-hour day, then we need a three-hour day. It all depends on our level of trust, the trust engrained in our basic personality.

The more we strive…

The more we strive to earn our way through life, the better we can understand that our wealth comes only from the heavens – and the stronger is our trust. Such a trust, together with prayer and patience, may then bring us our hearts' desires.

Our Perception

Trust depends on our perception, the level of our belief. When we are at a higher level of trust, we need to take care not to do too much. When we are at a lower level, we must be careful to do enough.*

Belief

The more we believe a certain something is coming our way, the sooner it will come. Why then do we work for what we want? – Only to overcome the deficiency of inadequate belief.

Keep this rule in mind: When we see it coming, it's coming.34

---

* Rav Yosef Chaim Zonnenfeld as a student was penniless and lived frugally. When he really needed money, he would take a walk in the streets and after a few blocks find a gold napoleon. This happened a number of times. Once, however, he went walking thus looking at the ground as he walked, and a man stopped him. "Excuse me," he said to Rav Yosef Chaim, "did you lose something here?" Rav Yosef Chaim blushed. He had been caught putting his trust into perceived circumstances rather than into the Creator.

Giving

Basic to our trust is that we know that whatever money or gifts we give to others, will return to us and we will lose nothing by our gift.[35] Moreover, once we break through the giving barrier, besides not losing from our generosity, on the contrary, we will become only the richer.

I give you my heart

Connect

Think about the Creator. Focus on the Creator. See the Creator all around you. Close your eyes and speak with the Creator, and have him speak back to you.

A Deeper Connection

We all at times, feel helpless, hopeless. We should use these times however, to deepen our connection with the One who listens to all prayers, and answers all prayers.

A Door

Have you ever tried breaking through a wall, only to discover hours later that there is an open doorway just a few steps away? We must pray constantly for guidance.

Born To Be

Here's a powerful request to add to our daily prayers:

"Help me, please, to be the person I was born to be."

Eyes that See

Everything we could possibly want is already right around us – there for the taking. The problem is though we can't see it. Let us strive and pray then for eyes that see.

No Snacking

We don't snack before going to the king's banquet; we know that every delicacy to fill every hunger will be there. Similarly, when we pray, we should come with empty hands – we should leave our luggage behind. In this way, we know, we will come away with multiple gifts and blessings.

Not then, now

Don't simply pray for something you hope will happen sometime in the future. Rather, let your prayer make it a reality within yourself right now.

Pray Away

Turn what bothers you into a prayer – pray that the problem goes away. Then, while you're praying for something small, pray for something magnificent as well.

Three-Way Formula

Here is a three-way formula to connect us with the Creator:

Past: Forgive me my carelessness and the wrongs that sprang from them.

Future: Help me succeed and achieve my heart's wishes.

Present: Thank You for life, the goodness You grant me today, and every day.

In short, we need to say and keep saying: **Forgive me. Help me. Thank You.**

Waiting and Praying

Often our worst problems "fix themselves" by us simply waiting and praying, and waiting some more, and praying some more, and nothing else.

Despite it all

A Solution

When we feel a little down, we can attribute this to a build up in our system of negative thoughts, words and actions. The junk we have accumulated is now rising to the surface and making us miserable. One solution is to turn our mind to the heavens and call out, "Please, forgive me, clear me, cleanse me, please…"

Ask for Help

When we ask for help, the Creator helps us. When we don't ask for help, He also helps us. He helps us to ask for help.

Booster

A great energy booster for when we're feeling low is to take a few deep breaths. And, when we accompany these breaths with beautiful thoughts, they become even more powerful.

No Other

Our lives include the sweet and the bitter, the easy and the difficult, the inspiring and the boring. All these elements together benefit us – complement each other and teach us to grow. This process becomes the smoother when we remember and repeat to ourselves that one source of energy generates all life – there is "No Other Besides [the Creator]".[36]

Obstacles

Obstacles prevent us advancing along our life path as quickly as we would like to move. The key to removing these obstacles though, lies within us. With a little humility, a little gratitude, we clear the path before us.[37]

The Right Way

It's not enough to know the right way; we have also to practice it, many times over, until it becomes a part of ourselves.

Try again

If we get it wrong, let's try – for next time – to get it right.

Your Enemy

Think of the person who most hurt you, embarrassed and robbed you. Now, direct feelings of warm, wonderful love and respect towards this same person. You will find that this empowers you in an awesome way.[38]

Mostly

Mostly, we're better off not punishing or revenging ourselves against those who hurt us. Mostly, we're better off ignoring our grievance at the wrong done to us. If we can be strong and wise, we do ourselves the greatest favor of all by just forgetting all about it.[39]

Friends, Enemies

Best friends become enemies when matched in a game against each other. This is the nature of games. We have to realize that likewise, the challenges of life are part of a game – to help draw out our hidden potential and enrich us.

Innermost, Deepest

Our innermost, deepest desires are the most beautiful and powerful desires we have. Often though, it takes a "heartbreaking" event for us to realize that they've been there all along.[40]

Highlights

We imagine the highlights of our life to be public events, a wedding or a child's wedding, a promotion or a new purchase. But, the real highlights are the breakthroughs we make in connecting with the Source of all Life and including it in our reality.

Glow

To glow, turn the light on within yourself.

Fill the Gap

A large gap exists between what our world has given us and what we have given in return. We need to think this over seriously. It will motivate us to do much more.[41]

Extra-Ordinary

Instead of being ordinary, let's be extra-ordinary. Let's put more heart into all that we do.

Endnotes

1 Chochma v'Mussar vol.2 essay 92

2 The Torah commands us to love our neighbor as ourselves (VaYikra 19.18), as well as to love the Creator with our entirety (Devarim 6.5).

3 "*Sachel*" is that part of the intellect that converts thoughts into actions. "*Chamor*" the Hebrew word for a donkey, also refers to the physical matter of this world. We have the potential to control the physical world with our minds. Based on Shiurei Daas 3.1

4 In the way, a person wishes to go, they [the heavens] direct him. (Makkos 10b)

5 Brochos 32b

6 Shaarei Teshuva 1.27

7 Based on Mishle 21.8

8 Devarim 20.19

9 Based on Mishle 18.1

10 "In the way, a person wishes to, he is lead..." (Makkos 10b)

11 Based on Shiurei Daas 3.1

12 Based on Daas Torah, Shmos p. 265

13 Based on the verse, "the upright lives with his faith" - Chabakuk 2.4

14 Based on the verse, "Let not the wise person glory in his wisdom, nor the mighty person in his might, nor the rich person glory in his riches; But let him that take glory, glory in this, that he understands and knows Me..." (Yermiyahu 9.22)

15 Attributed to Rav Yisrael Salanter.

[16] Based on Koheles 9.10

[17] Based on Shaarei Teshuva 1.27; Sanhedrin 99a

[18] Mishle 10.24

[19] Based on Tehillim 40.2 and Mishle 20.22

[20] Based on Mishle 28.12 as explained by Rabbeinu Yona, Shaarei Teshuva 1.18

[21] All your deeds should be for the sake of heaven – Pirkei Avos 2.12

[22] The verse says, "Walk modestly with Hashem…" (Micha 6.8); this tells us that when we act in a modest way, then we are with Hashem, and He is with us.

[23] Chochma v'Mussar 1.65

[24] Based on Mishna Torah, Hilchos Teshuva 3.7

[25] The Torah lifestyle is "the pleasant way" (Mishle 3.17)

[26] Based on Mishle 11.17

[27] One who forgives the wrongdoings of others, the heavens, in turn, overlook his sins… (Rosh HaShana 17a)

[28] They came, every one whose heart stirred him, every one whose spirit prompted him … Shmos 35.21

[29] Based on Mishle 21.10

[30] Based on Alei Shur vol.2 p.577

[31] This was King David's focal point, as he wrote, "…to You are all my desires; I don't hide my longing from you" (Tehillim 35.10) – based on Shaarei Teshuva 1.14

[32] Based on Tehillim 10.4

[33] Breishis Raba 2.2. See "Wealth - A Torah Approach" by this author p.66

34 There are number of references to "bitachon", the trust or certainty which Hashem honors. Maybe the most well-known is "One who trusts in Hashem [that He will show him kindness], is surrounded by kindness" (Tehillim 32.10). The idea that the more we trust in Hashem, the more He honors our trust, is a logical idea, which is powefully illustrated by a famous teaching/story from Rav Chaim Volozhiner (brought in Keep Smiling p.163)

35 Rav Chaim of Volozhin writes: I heard from my Rebbe (the Vilna Gaon) that one who gives 10% of his income to charity will suffer no loss, while one who gives 20% will become wealthy ... for he has strengthened his trust ... – Siddur HaGra, Keser Rosh.

36 Devarim 4.35

37 Based on Yeshayahu 57.14,15

38 All hurt we suffer comes from the Creator ... For you own peace of mind...

39 Based on VaYikra 19.18

40 Shaarei Teshuva 1.33

41 Based on Shaarei Teshuva 1.25

www.ingramcontent.com/pod-product-compliance
Lightning Source LLC
LaVergne TN
LVHW021600070426
835507LV00014B/1880